A NOTE TO PARENTS

When your children are ready to "step into reading," giving them the right books is as crucial as giving them the right food to eat. **Step into Reading Books** present exciting stories and information reinforced with lively, colorful illustrations that make learning to read fun, satisfying, and worthwhile. They are priced so that acquiring an entire library of them is affordable. And they are beginning readers with a difference—they're written on five levels.

Early Step into Reading Books are designed for brand-new readers, with large type and only one or two lines of very simple text per page. **Step 1 Books** feature the same easy-to-read type as the Early Step into Reading Books, but with more words per page. **Step 2 Books** are both longer and slightly more difficult, while **Step 3 Books** introduce readers to paragraphs and fully developed plot lines. **Step 4 Books** offer exciting nonfiction for the increasingly independent reader.

The grade levels assigned to the five steps—preschool through kindergarten for the Early Books, preschool through grade 1 for Step 1, grades 1 through 3 for Step 2, grades 2 through 3 for Step 3, and grades 2 through 4 for Step 4—are intended only as guides. Some children move through all five steps very rapidly; others climb the steps over a period of several years. Either way, these books will help your child "step into reading" in style!

http://www.randomhouse.com/

POLLY POCKET and associated characters are registered trademarks of Bluebird Toys (UK) Ltd., England.

Library of Congress Cataloging-in-Publication Data:
Albert, Shirley. The Polly Pocket cookbook / by Shirley Albert ; illustrated by Emilie Kong.
p. cm. — (Step into reading. A step 2 book) "Grades 1–3"—CIP cover. SUMMARY: Polly Pocket and her friends present easy-to-follow recipes for some of their favorite foods, including Strawberry Waffles, Banana Bites, and Tuna Treats. ISBN 0-679-87484-4 (pbk.) — ISBN 0-679-97484-9 (lib. bdg.) 1. Cookery—Juvenile literature. [1. Cookery.] I. Kong, Emilie, ill. II. Title. III. Series. TX652.5.A43 1996 641.5'123—dc20 96-13578

Printed in the United States of America 10 9 8 7 6 5 4 3 2 1

STEP INTO READING is a trademark of Random House, Inc.

Step into Reading™

The Polly Pocket® Cookbook

by Shirley Albert
illustrated by Emilie Kong

A Step 2 Book

Random House New York

I'm Polly Pocket.

I'm the very best cook

in Pollyville.

My sisters, my brother,

and my friends

all love to cook.

We make our favorite foods:

strawberry waffles,

vanilla shakes—

even tasty tuna treats!

You can learn how to cook, too!

Follow these easy recipes.

Then have your own

Polly Pocket party!

Polly's Kitchen Rules

Everyone has to follow

my kitchen rules.

They are as easy as ABC and 1, 2, 3!

1. Always make sure a grownup

is home when you cook.

2. Clear a space so you have

lots of room to work.

3. Read the recipe

all the way through.

Then gather together

everything you need.

What else?

4. Wash your hands.
Wear an apron.

5. You won't need
an oven.
But you will need
a knife and an eggbeater.
Sometimes you will have
to use a toaster oven
or a can opener.
Always ask a
grownup
for help.

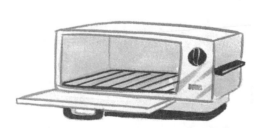

6. Don't forget to clean up

when you are done!

Polly's Cooking Tips

This is a
tablespoon.

This is a
teaspoon.
See? It's smaller.

This is a measuring cup.

See the marks on the side?

They tell you

different measurements.

Tina is my little sister.

She loves an adventure.

Especially in the kitchen!

Let's see what she stirs up.

♥ Ask a grownup for help!

You will need:

½ teaspoon of sugar

½ teaspoon of cinnamon

1 slice of bread

1 pat of butter

bowl

spoon

toaster (And a grownup's help!)

butter knife

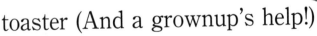

How to make it:

1. Put the sugar in the bowl.

2. Add the cinnamon.

3. Mix them together.

The cinnamon-sugar should be

a nice brown color!

4. Toast the bread.

(Ask a grownup for help!)

5. Spread butter on the toast.

6. Sprinkle some cinnamon-sugar on top.

This toast is just as sweet as Tina!

Lulu is my other sister.

She is quiet and shy.

But she will tell you a secret:

How to make

her favorite breakfast!

Lulu's Strawberry Waffles

♥ Ask a grownup for help!

You will need:

1 pint of strawberries

2 teaspoons of sugar

2 frozen waffles

butter knife

cutting board

bowl

spoon

eggbeater

toaster (And a grownup's help!)

How to make it:

1. Wash the strawberries.

Carefully cut off the tops.

2. Cut each strawberry in half.

Put the slices in a bowl.

Mash them down

with the back of the spoon.

3. Add the sugar.

4. Mix the strawberries and sugar
all together with an eggbeater.

5. Ask a grownup to help you
toast two frozen waffles.

6. Spoon the strawberries
on top.

Willie is my little brother.

He plays sports.

He runs and jumps

and rolls around.

And he loves this

roll-around snack!

Wee Willie's Roll-Up

You will need:

5 shelled walnuts

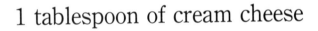

1 slice of bread

1 tablespoon of cream cheese

1 tablespoon of jelly

plastic sandwich bag

spoon

butter knife

cutting board

toothpick

How to make it:

1. Place the walnuts in the bag.
Close it tight.

2. Press down with the spoon
to crush the nuts into little pieces.
Put them aside.

3. Carefully cut the crust off the bread.

4. Flatten the bread with the
back of the spoon.

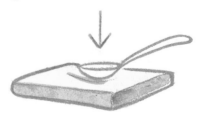

5. Spread the cream cheese and jelly on the bread.

6. Sprinkle crushed walnuts on top.

7. Roll the bread into a log shape.

8. Carefully stick a toothpick in the middle.

Sometimes Willie needs a cool break.

His super-duper shake

really hits the spot!

Willie's Super-Duper Shake

You will need:

1 banana

½ cup of milk

½ cup of soft frozen vanilla yogurt
  or vanilla ice cream

2 teaspoons of honey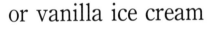

bowl

spoon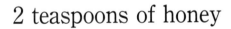

eggbeater

2 glasses

How to make it:

1. Peel the banana.

Mash it in the bowl

with the back of the spoon.

2. Pour in the milk.

3. Scoop in the yogurt.

4. Drizzle in the honey.

5. Mix it all together

with the eggbeater.

Is the mixture smooth?

Good! You're done!

Pour the shake into two glasses.

My pal Diddy makes us a special treat, too.

His mini-pizzas are delicious!

♥ Ask a grownup for help!

You will need:

1 English muffin

3 tablespoons of tomato sauce

2 tablespoons of grated
   mozzarella cheese

spoon

toaster oven (And a
   grownup's help!)

How to make it:

1. Split the English muffin in half.

2. Spoon the tomato sauce

on the muffin halves.

3. Sprinkle the cheese on top.

4. Ask a grownup to help you toast the muffin halves. Place the mini-pizzas on the toaster tray. When the cheese is melted, they're done!

What do *I* like to cook?

Extra-special Polly Pocket meals!

You will need:

1 banana

2 tablespoons of peanut butter

1 apple

1 pita

bowl

spoon

eggbeater

knife

cutting board

How to make it:

1. Peel the banana.
Mash it in the bowl
with the back
of the spoon.

2. Add the peanut butter.

3. Mix them together
with the eggbeater.
Put the mixture aside
for now.

4. Wash the apple.
Ask a grownup to
peel and cut the apple
into little pieces.

5. Cut the pita in half.
Now you have two pockets.

6. Spread the peanut butter mixture inside the pockets.

7. Then stuff the sandwiches with apple pieces.

Polly's
Tuna Treat

♥Ask
a grownup
for help!

Want another pocket pleaser?

Here is a tasty tuna treat!

You will need:

1 can of tuna fish

1½ tablespoons of mayonnaise

1 pita

can opener

bowl

fork

butter knife

cutting board

How to make it:

1. Ask a grownup
to open the tuna can
and drain the liquid.

2. Mash the tuna in a bowl
with a fork.

3. Add the mayonnaise.
Mix and mash
until the tuna is smooth.

4. Carefully cut the top off

the pita bread.

Fill it with your tuna treat!

Midge grows fruits and vegetables.

She's bananas about bananas!

You will need:

1 banana

10 shelled walnuts

1 cup of rice cereal

2 teaspoons of honey

bowl

spoon

plastic sandwich bag

ice cube tray

toothpicks

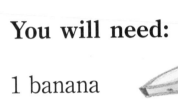

How to make it:

1. Peel the banana.
Then mash it in the bowl
with the back of the spoon.

2. Put the walnuts in the bag.
Close it tight.
Press down with the spoon
to crush the nuts into little pieces.

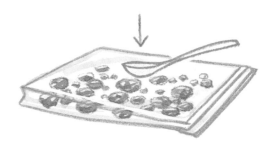

3. Add the nuts to the bowl.
Now pour in the cereal.

4. Drizzle in the honey
and mix it all together.

5. Spoon the mixture into the ice cube tray.

6. Carefully stick toothpicks into every cube.

7. Place the tray in the freezer. Leave it there for one hour.

8. Scoop out your banana bites!

My friend Pixie is an artist.

Her yummy desserts are always

pretty as a picture!

You will need:

1 small orange

2 dessert shells

½ cup of whipped cream

¼ cup of orange juice

bowl

spoon

How to make it:

1. Peel the orange. Separate the pieces.

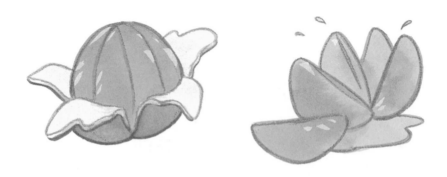

2. Place the pieces
in the dessert shells.

3. Scoop all the whipped cream into
the bowl.

4. Pour the juice into the bowl.

Now mix.

The whipped cream
should stay fluffy.

5. Spoon the whipped cream

and juice on top

of the orange pieces.

A masterpiece!

Partytime, everyone!